Aphorisms

for the

Uncommon Reader

William Melvin Gardner

Logica Books

L
B

Cover art by Susan Patton

Published by Logica Books
PO Box 111
Fairhope, AL 36532
USA

ISBN 978-0-9761875-3-0

APHORISMS AND APHORISTS

The word *aphorism* can be traced back more than two thousand years to the Greek word *aphorismos* (ἀφορισμός), meaning definition, delimitation, or distinction. In 400 BC Hippocrates summarized his medical knowledge with a list of instructive aphorisms, the first of which is still relevant:

> Life is short, and art long; the crisis fleeting; experience perilous, and decision difficult. The physician must not only be prepared to do what is right himself, but also to make the patient, the attendants, and externals cooperate.

In modern scholarly usage, the term *aphorism* is generally reserved for insightful comments that are brief and witty. There are many other words with similar meanings, and in common usage the distinctions are often blurred. The definitions and examples below offer some clarification of the word *aphorism*, vis-à-vis similar terms.

Adage An old familiar saying, often metaphorical: "Out of sight, out of mind." —John Heywood

Aphorism An observation, instruction, or definition, distinguished by its brevity, wit, insight, sweeping implications, and a twist: "To have a knife at your enemy's throat—what a dangerous moment!" —Stanislaw J. Lec

Apothegm A practical, pithy saying, often in the form of instruction or advice: "Never put off until tomorrow what you can do today." — Benjamin Franklin

Epigram A short, satirical, amusing, and memorable poem or remark that addresses a specific circumstance or subject: "Candy is dandy, but liquor is quicker." — Ogden Nash

Maxim An axiomatic saying, practical advice, or commonsense principle: "What goes up must come down." —Isaac Newton

Paradox An assertion or instruction that contradicts or contravenes itself, often for the sake of irony: "We have met the enemy and he is us." —Walt Kelly

Pensée An insightful reflection, description, thought, or metaphor: "When the topmost palm leaves are shaken by the wind their shadows on the ground keep clicking their heels." —Malcolm de Chazal

Platitude A trite bromide or mollifying cliché: "Everything happens for a reason." — Unknown

Proverb A simple and popular saying (often a parallelism) supporting morals or cultural values: "When the going gets tough, the tough get going." —Joseph P. Kennedy (and Knute Rockne)

> *Witticism* A witty, targeted remark intended to amuse: "I have been told that Wagner's music is better than it sounds." —Edgar Wilson Nye

Among these overlapping terms, aphorisms are the most likely to be philosophical, provocative, original, and attributed, and because of their attribution they are often listed under the generic heading, "Quotes," and all too often misattributed.

As can be seen in Ambrose Bierce's *The Devil's Dictionary* (1911), aphorisms are often cynical or contrary to popular opinion, for example "Bride, *n.* A woman with a fine prospect of happiness behind her." The most enticing characteristic of an aphorism is, however, its ability to surprise, stimulate thought, and provide a fresh perspective. In Stanislaw J. Lec's *Unkempt Thoughts* (1962) aphorisms such as "The first condition of immortality is death" may leave the thoughtful reader a bit unsettled.

Aphorisms may appear wise, but they are typically just witty assertions that challenge popular wisdom. Author and critic Clifton Fadiman wrote in his introduction to Lec's *Unkempt Thoughts*: "An aphorism (this one of course excepted) can contain only as much wisdom as overstatement will permit."

Aphorisms are typically written as stand-alone assertions, but many have been discovered lurking in poems, plays, speeches, letters, essays, and novels. "The past is never dead. It is not even past." appears in William Faulkner's *Requiem for a Nun*.

Most aphorisms are rarely quoted, and the resulting obscurity allows them to retain their freshness. On the other hand, a few often-repeated aphorisms have become little more than adages. Consider how often we hear some variant of John Dalberg-Acton's observation, "Power tends to corrupt, and absolute power corrupts absolutely," or George Santayana's warning, "Those who cannot remember the past are condemned to repeat it."

The reader who wants to know more about aphorisms and aphorists has a choice of sources: anthologies such as *The Viking Book of Aphorisms, A Personal Selection* (1966, 1993) by W. H. Auden and Louis Kronenberger; *Oxford Book of Aphorisms* (1983) by John Gross; and *Geary's Guide to the World's Great Aphorists* (2007) by James Geary, as well as websites such as *aphorism4all* and *aphorismsgalore*. There are also reviews of the works of selected aphorists, for example *The World in a Phrase: A Brief History of The Aphorism* (2005) by James Geary and *Short Flights: Thirty-Two Modern Writers Share Aphorisms of Insight, Inspiration, and Wit* (2015) edited by James Lough and Alex Stein.

Few of the aphorists featured in anthologies and reviews are women, but that may be changing. Lily

Akerman, Sharon Dolin, Olivia Dresher, Irena Karafilly, Ann Lauinger, Sara Levine, and Holly Woodward are among the contemporary writers whose aphorisms appear in Lough and Stein's *Short Flights*. These women provide some the best aphorisms in the collection, and Irena Karafilly's works place her among the best aphorists of our times, for example "People are at their most brilliant while defending themselves against their own conscience" and "The only power you have over other people is the ability to do without them."

Anthologies tend to feature aphorisms by writers who are recognized by their surname or cognomen alone: Bacon, Baudelaire, Blake, Chamfort, Chekhov, Chesterton, Churchill, Confucius, Diderot, Diogenes, Disraeli, Emerson, Goethe, Halifax, Huxley, Kierkegaard, La Rochefoucauld, Lavater, Lichtenberg, Mencken, Montaigne, Montesquieu, Nietzsche, Pascal, Pope, Pound, Proust, Santayana, Schopenhauer, Seneca, Shakespeare, Shaw, Swift, Tacitus, Thoreau, Tocqueville, Twain, Valéry, Voltaire, Wilde, Wittgenstein, and many others. These celebrated thinkers rarely authored books of aphorisms, but from just before until just after the Age of Enlightenment there were at least a few who did. These books include Blaise Pascal's *Pensées* (1660), François Duc de La Rochefoucauld's *Réflexions; ou, sentences et maximes morales* (1665), Johann Kaspar Lavater's *Aphorisms on Man* (1787), and Georg Christoph Lichtenberg's *Vermischte Schriften* (1800). The substance and style of La Rochefoucauld's and Lichtenberg's aphorisms inspired and influenced many of the aphorists who followed.

Over the period extending from the beginning of the twentieth century until today, several writers produced books of aphorisms. Prominent among these prolific aphorists are Ambrose Bierce, Antonio Porchia, Malcolm de Chazal, Eric Hoffer, Stanislaw J. Lec, Mikhail Turovsky, James Richardson, Yahia Lababidi, James Guida, JPJ, Nassim Nicholas Taleb, and George Murray. A brief introduction to the life and works of each is presented below.

Ambrose Gwinnett Bierce was born in Ohio in 1842 and came of age just in time to serve in the Union Army during the Civil War. After his distinguished military service, Bierce's life took many unusual and eventful turns, but in time he established himself as a columnist, critic, and fiction writer. He is remembered today as the battle-hardened Civil War veteran who wrote a body of fiction based on his experiences with the horrors and psychological fog of that brutal war. Three of his short stories, "An Occurrence at Owl Creek Bridge," "Chickamauga," and "Jupiter Doke, Brigadier-

General" exemplify his talent as a creative writer. His aphorisms first appeared in 1881 in "The Devil's Dictionary" column in *The Wasp,* a satirical American magazine published in San Francisco, but it was thirty years later, near the end of his life, when *The Devil's Dictionary,* a book of mordant and cynical definitions and poems, was published. This still popular work contains several hundred definitional aphorisms that reveal Bierce's intellect as well as his dry and unsmiling sense of humor. For example: "Pray, *v.* To ask that the laws of the universe be annulled in behalf of a single petitioner confessedly unworthy" and "Vote, *n.* The instrument and symbol of a freeman's power to make a fool of himself and a wreck of his country." In December of 1913 Bierce disappeared, perhaps intentionally, into war-torn Mexico and was presumed to have been killed there, but biographers have proposed other theories. *The Devil's Dictionary* has been republished many times over the last century, and it remains in publication today.

Antonio Porchia was born in Southern Italy in 1886. His father died when he was twelve, and Antonio received only a basic education before beginning work at age fourteen. His mother moved with her children to Beunos Aires, Argentina, where Antonio and his younger brothers eventually entered the printing business. He retired in 1936, and in 1943 he privately published *Voces,* his book of aphorisms. His aphorisms attracted a local following, and in 1949 Roger Caillois translated many of them from Spanish to French. Just before Porchia's death in 1968, W. S. Merwin began work on an English translation. Merwin's translation, *Voices,* was published in 1969. A revised and enlarged edition was published in 1988, and in 2003 it was republished in a Spanish/English linear translation. In his retirement Porchia lived a simple, solitary life and was not known to have read widely, yet many readers see eastern religious thought in his serene, introspective, and occasionally enigmatic aphorisms. Consider the following two examples, "When you and truth speak to me, I do not listen to truth. I listen to you" and "Because they know the name of what I am looking for, they think they know what I am looking for!"

Malcolm de Chazal was a visionary writer and painter, born to a French-speaking family in Mauritius in 1902. After receiving an engineering degree from Louisiana State University and Agricultural and Mechanical College, he returned to Mauritius where he was employed as an agronomist. He later worked at the Office of Telecommunications. His book of sensuous metaphors, reflections, and aphorisms,

Pensées et Sens-plastique, was published in 1945. The Gallimard edition of *Sens-Plastique, Volume II*, published in 1948, brought Chazal acclaim in France. *Sens-Plastique* was translated from French to English by Irving Weiss and published in 1971, then republished twice, first in 1979 and again in 2008. Chazal died in 1981, leaving his readers thousands of sensuous pensées and aphorisms such as "A man's heart lies in his sex; a woman's sex lies in her heart," and "No fig leaves can ever hide your lips and mouth."

Eric Hoffer was born to a German-speaking family in New York City in 1898 and died in San Francisco in 1983. When he was seven years old his mother died as a result of a fall she had suffered two years earlier. Her death led to Hoffer's loss of vision and, for a time, his memory. At age fifteen, after his vision inexplicably returned, he became a voracious reader. When his father died, Hoffer moved to California where he spent years on skid row taking odd jobs and eventually became a migrant worker. He was rejected for military service at the outset of World War II but found work as a longshoreman on the San Francisco docks. He became well known for his 1951 book *The True Believer: Thoughts on the Nature of Mass Movements*. His book of aphorisms, *The Passionate State of Mind ~ and other aphorisms*, was published in 1955. Unlike most aphorists,

10

Hoffer had a central theme: "Faith in a holy cause is to a considerable extent a substitute for the lost faith in ourselves." His aphorisms provide insights into human motives, passions, and self-deceptions. Many are short and powerful, for instance, "The fear of becoming a 'has been' keeps some people from becoming anything." Other longer ones seem to be progressions of related aphorisms: "To be truly selfish one needs a degree of self-esteem. The self-despisers are less intent on their own increase than on the diminution of others. Where self-esteem is unattainable, envy takes the place of greed."

Stanislaw Jerzy Lec was born Baron Stanislaw Jerzu de Tusch-Letz in 1909 in Lviv, Austria-Hungary, and died in Warsaw, Poland, in 1966. During World War II, he was among the many Polish Jews imprisoned and facing possible execution, a fate he avoided by donning a German soldier's uniform in order to escape. He subsequently joined the communist branch of the Polish resistance, and later the Polish People's Army, but by 1950 he had become disillusioned with communist government. Lec's first book of aphorisms, *Myśli nieuczesane*, was published in 1957. It was translated from Polish to English by Jacek Galazka and in 1962 published in the U.S. with the English title *Unkempt Thoughts*. A companion book,

More Unkempt Thoughts, was published posthumously in 1968. Lec set a benchmark against which future aphorists and aphorisms could be measured. Clifton Fadiman's introduction to *Unkempt Thoughts* provides an extensive and scholarly review of aphorisms and aphorists, reserving special praise for Lec's beguiling and thought-provoking aphorisms, such as "On the neck of a giraffe a flea begins to believe in immortality" and "'I feel I am growing wings,' said the mouse. 'So what, bat?'"

Michail Turovsky was born in Kiev in 1933 during Joseph Stalin's "terror famine" in which Soviet economic policies led to the starvation of millions of Ukrainians. In the 1960s Turovsky earned his M.F.A. from the Kiev State Art Institute. He subsequently received a Ph.D. from the USSR Academy of Art, and became a well-known artist before immigrating to New York City in 1979. Many of his paintings memorialize the human suffering brought on by the Holocaust. Turovsky's book of aphorisms, *Зуд Мудрости,* was published in 1981. It was translated from Russian to English by Edmund Levin and Lilia Rogovaia in 1986 and published in 1990 with the title *Itch of Wisdom.* While Turovsky's aphorisms lack the cynical bite of Bierce's and the guile and charm of Lec's, many of them provide intellectual and witty insights into the individual's struggle against oppression and injustice. For instance, "Everybody keeps quiet for his own reasons" and "Give me Freedom! I want to get disillusioned with it for myself."

James Richardson graduated from Princeton University in 1971 and earned his Ph.D. from the University of Virginia in 1975. In 1980 he returned to Princeton where he currently serves as Professor of English and Creative Writing. His work includes a book of aphorisms, *Vectors: Aphorisms & Ten-Second Essays* (2001), and two books with many additional aphorisms, *Interglacial: New and Selected Poems & Aphorisms* (2004) and *By the Numbers: Poems and Aphorisms* (2010). Richardson's aphorisms are dependably original, captivating, and thought provoking, and more than a few reveal the soul of a poet, as can be seen in "The head learns quickly and forgets. The heart learns slowly and, since it cannot forget, must betray itself to move on" and "The days are in order, the months, the seasons, the years. But weeks are work. They have no names; they repeat." As the title *Vectors: Aphorisms & Ten-Second Essays* suggests, his aphoristic writings vary widely in length, from brief assertions to long paragraphs.

Yahia Lababidi is a celebrated Egyptian-American poet who was born in 1978 and came to the U.S. in 1996.

He began writing aphorisms while still a student at George Washington University. His book, *Signposts to Elsewhere: A book of aphorisms, epigrams, maxims and other tailored thoughts*, was published in 2006. A second book of aphorisms, *Where Epics Fail: Meditations To Live By*, was published in 2018. Lababidi's aphorisms reflect his subtle and sensitive view of life, for example, "We are cruelest when we ought to be kindest—when someone is losing a battle, or war, which we've waged and won before."

James Guida is a journalist and non-fiction writer. He was born in Philadelphia in 1978 but grew up in Australia. He now lives in New York City and is well known for his essays published in the *New York Review of Books*. His book of aphorisms, *Marbles,* was published in 2009, and in 2011 The New York Foundation for the Arts awarded him a fellowship in non-fiction. His longer aphorisms require reader persistence, for example, "When the news came—that, from the Sublime, Ridiculousness might be reached by a single step—an assembly was called, and soon reached a decision. A great wall was to be built in front of the Sublime. Ahead of the wall, in turn, would be a sharp ditch. A flag would mark the boundary." His shorter aphorisms, however, can be engaging and direct, for instance, "Countless worries sometimes don't add up to a single vicissitude."

JPJ's collection, *Last Aphorisms*, was self-published in 2009. The book provides neither a copyright page nor the author's name. According to two websites, *acronymattic* and *aphorismsgalore*, JPJ's name is Jeremy Preston Johnson. Whoever he is, his aphorisms are remarkably brief, clear, insightful, and clever. The following examples illustrate his talent: "The Devil has attracted many because, unlike god, he is willing to negotiate" and "Death insures that something interesting happens in our lives." JPJ's book inspires a new aphorism: "Pure genius is anonymous."

Nassim Nicholas Taleb was born in Lebanon in 1960 and grew up during the Lebanese Civil War. He studied at the University of Paris, where he received his bachelor's degree and master's. He went on to earn an MBA at the Wharton School of the University of Pennsylvania and then returned to the University of Paris where he received a PhD in Management Science. Taleb is well known for his best seller *The Black Swan* (2007). A lesser-known book, *The Bed of Procrustes: Philosophical and Practical Aphorisms*, was published in 2010. Many of Taleb's aphorisms are haughty critiques: "If you can't spontaneously detect (without analyzing) the difference between sacred and profane, you'll never know what religion means. You will also never figure out what we commonly call art. You will never understand anything." Others are thoughtful insights: "It is harder to say *no* when you really mean it than when you don't."

George Murray was born in Canada in 1971 and spent several years abroad, first in Italy and then in New York City. In 2005 he returned to Canada where he was named poet laureate of St. John's, Newfoundland and Labrador. He has written books of poetry and held editorial positions with literary journals. Murray's book of aphorisms, *Glimpse: Selected Aphorisms*, was published in 2010. The examples that follow show his special talent for brevity, insight, and wit, as well as his ability to amuse and entertain readers: "Panic is worry on a tight schedule" and "Writing the erotic poem is like ironing in the nude—sexy for women, dangerous for men."

*   *   *   *   *

Composing the hundreds of aphorisms needed for publication as a personal collection may take a lifetime of thinking, crafting, and revising. Even then, because good aphorisms are often provocative and intellectually demanding, the market for a collection will always be limited to the uncommon reader.

16

In the following excerpt from the poem *Let's Not Play Lotto, Let's Talk* presented in *Verses from 1929 On* published in 1952, Ogden Nash laments the absence of aphorisms in social conversation:

Take the causerie of the most effervescent coterie,

It sounds like something sworn to before a notary.

Where are yesterday's epigrams, banter and badinage?

All you hear is who behaved scandalously at the club dance and how hard it is to get a new car into an old garage.

The maxim, the apothegm, yea, even the aphorism, die like echoes in the distance,

Overwhelmed by such provocative topics as clothes, beauticians, taxes and the scarcity of competent domestic assistants.   *(Curtis Brown LTD)*

Witty conversationalists and successful aphorists are thinkers who are at their best when they possess a resilient intellect, a social conscience, good humor, and a pithiness of expression—as well as a direct knowledge of the folly, hypocrisy, and cruelty in human affairs. In the introduction to *Rubaiyat of Omar Khayyam* (1948) Louis Untermeyer quotes the translator Edward FitzGerald's apt description of the nature and work of the thinker, and thus the aphorist: "... a desperate sort of thing at the bottom of all thinking men's minds! But the tune is so gay that even the pessimism seems blithe."

Aphorists don't choose their craft. They are conversationalists and writers whose ideas and insights naturally reduce to aphorisms. When hundreds of well-honed aphorisms accumulate, friends ask, "Why don't you do something with them?" When the aphorisms are finally published, the uncommon readers may feel that they have discovered a new friend, someone who shares their disinterest in "…such provocative topics as clothes, beauticians, taxes and the scarcity of competent domestic assistants."

18

APHORISMS
FOR THE
UNCOMMON READER

We make lifelong friends while we are young and indiscriminate.

While both eyes of the predator aim toward the prey, one eye of the prey is aimed at the predator and one in the opposite direction.

College provides asylum from the tyranny of common sense.

Mortality: *n.* The characteristic that distinguishes the living from the dead.

We usually understand what we heard, even when we don't understand what was said.

"Anything is possible." We can't stop saying it, even though it's obviously false.

Moral: *adj.* Maintaining a positive regard for others, without making a distinction between the deserving and the undeserving.

Spouse: *n.* Someone who settled for what was available.

We are confused about our motives, especially after we have heard our justifications.

Jurors: *n. pl.* Citizens tasked with determining who is lying.

Voters: *n. pl.* Citizens tasked with determining who is telling the truth.

Wisdom allows us to make the right choice, but freedom allows us to make the wrong choice.

Inhumane acts of war were banned at the Geneva Conventions, thereby insuring that all future wars would be humane.

Partisanship: *n.* Commitment to half the facts and none of the reasoning.

By settling the score with offenders, victims add to their numbers.

Far more people weren't conceived than were.

Internet: *n.* An electronic system for bypassing editors.

If you must choose, hang on to your friends and let your enemies go.

For felony convictions, there must be proof of guilt of mind (*mens rea*) as well as guilt of body (*actus reus*), because the two cannot be separated for sentencing.

Perceptions*: n. pl.* Images from our past distorted to accommodate the objects currently before us.

Dictatorship: *n.* A democracy in which the incumbent leader receives over 90% of the vote.

Happiness isn't something that happens to us.
It's something we do.

Technology: *n.* Science's prodigal son.

Adult: *n.* Someone guided by the errors of
childhood.

Belief in the unknown grows to fill the void
created by ignorance of the known.

Capitalism: *n.* An ingenious system for creating
work for workers, wealth for the wealthy, and
poverty for the poor.

26

Advances in understanding rest on advances in understanding, all the way down.

Art by Anita Overton

Adulthood: *n.* The developmental stage in which we abandon our selves to become our lives.

Freedoms: *n. pl.* Permits to encroach.

Friendship: *n.* A reciprocal tolerance between two people, from which at least one benefits.

For diplomatic reasons, gods usually appear in human form.

Militia: *n.* An armed mob organized by shirt color—historically black or brown.

We live in others but exist only in ourselves.

When the ignorant make sense, it's because they don't realize what they are saying.

Aging: *n.* The process of learning don't-do-its.

The poor buy and the wealthy invest, and that alone prevents a reversal of fortune.

If the future never becomes the here and now, it wasn't the future.

You can learn what you have to say only by listening when you speak.

Populist: *n.* A politician who appeals to the unappealing.

God-given rights are granted under color of title.

In a world of poets, dictionaries would provide only metaphors.

Adjectives and adverbs are makeup and jewelry for sentences.

Gullible: *adj.* Trusting your own judgment.

Only in India have gods been able to survive in significant numbers.

When the situation is hopeless, hope is our first reaction.

Uneducated people hold the beliefs of ancient tribes, but without knowledge of the beliefs of ancient tribes.

Shy people back through life, looking for a way out.

For historians, the name *Hindenburg* brings to mind the most appalling disaster of the Twentieth Century. In 1933, Adolph Hitler was appointed Chancellor of Germany by President Paul von *Hindenburg*.

Art by G P Gardner

Our misunderstandings expose our naiveté—
and our motives.

Prioritizing: *n.* Deciding what you can put off
until you no longer remember why you needed
to do it.

Life after death is believed certain. Death after
life is certain.

Problem: *n.* A dilemma created by rejecting
solutions.

Life is biodegradable.

Wit: *n.* An old parlor game for which the rules have been lost.

We were a mutual support team. He helped me help him.

Why: *adv.* An interrogative used to elicit an excuse, usually lame, always false.

Ethnocentric: *adj.* Maintaining an objective view of the inferior customs and values of foreigners.

Homo sapiens: The species that language uses.

36

The most knowledgeable person knows only a minuscule part of all that is known.

Art by Susan Petton

The price of war is war. The price of peace is peace. Neither is cheap.

Beware! Your thoughts aren't private. We can see you thinking.

Why aren't violators allowed to pay the fine in advance?

A head filled with facts can hold more new facts than an empty one.

A hard-enough push will not move even a coward.

Surgeons make more fatal errors than do pilots.

The more you help others, the more dependent they become, and the more demanding you become.

The face of the earth changed more over the last century than over the previous ten thousand years, yet progress was agonizingly slow.

Predator and prey both remain quiet and still when the other comes near, but for different reasons.

The notion that people are either left-brained or right-brained is a half-brained idea.

I once met a psychiatric patient who claimed to be the Devil. I assumed that he was delusional until I read his case history.

Art by Anita Overton

Suicide: *n.* The most dramatic complaint.

University: *n.* A production line for packaging and labeling students for the market place.

Tolerance of imposition breeds mutual disrespect, but so does intolerance.

Death brings only the loss of a past that was already gone and of a future that never existed.

Post-truth Era: When the search for truth advanced to information gathering.

The struggle against the wilderness is almost over, and the humans are winning.

Diplomacy: *n.* The art of purchasing guns from your enemy.

Pleasure: *n.* A scenic shortcut through time.

We can ask, "Why am I?" but the answer may be a disappointment.

Our understanding is *only* human, so our bombs are *only* nuclear.

Thinker: *n.* A person who is found in thought.

Photograph by G P Gardner

A mind can do nothing without a person to make it up.

Distrust of research is a well-documented finding.

A warning to the gods: Fear man, for he has created and destroyed many gods before you.

We have the legal right to kill ourselves, just not intentionally.

When a placebo cures the ill, the active ingredient is self-deception.

Metaphors: *n. pl.* Pleasing illusions that escape the gravity of reality.

Legislature: *n.* A public forum where conservatives ask why, liberals ask why not, and moderates must provide the answers.

God has answered our prayers! Science can now heal the sick and the injured!

Theology: *n.* The quixotic struggle to reconcile faith with reason.

To become a good listener, stop asking questions.

Anarchist: *n.* A nihilist with a bomb.

Terrorist: *n.* A zealot with a bomb.

We can make our own decisions, but the consequences must be left to others.

If you understand life you won't search for its meaning.

Ask, "Do you hold beliefs that you would not change regardless of the evidence?" If they answer "Yes," don't bother presenting evidence.

Hangover: *n.* A religious experience that dispels the fear of death.

Most people who could have developed the mental skills to become a genius didn't.

Literal: *adj.* The inability to fly by the seat of your pants.

Aphorism: *n.* The briefest and broadest form of the literary arts.

Many people are everything they claim to be as well as many other things they don't claim to be.

Failure calls for a new plan, success a new goal.

Confidant: *n.* An enemy in waiting.

Art by Susan Patton

We progress from disappointing our father and embarrassing our mother to disappointing our spouse and embarrassing our children.

We can remember what we know long past the time when we still knew it.

Jazz: *n.* A musical form that very few at first learn to play, but many at last learn to play.

Friendless: *adj.* Having no one left to ask you for help.

Agnostic: *n.* A skeptic who holds that anything is possible, even the preposterous.

People who believe the truth is a lie cannot learn the truth.

Opinions and beliefs, by their nature, need be neither factual nor rational.

The black widow spider romances his date, then pays for her dinner.

Consequences: *n. pl.* Our most tireless and persuasive teacher.

"In the beginning was The Word." Our Creator was Language!

Looks don't matter—unless they are noticed.

Art by Anita Overton

We can't see our understanding because it is the lens through which we see everything.

A person who succeeds in escaping to freedom will soon escape from freedom.

When you must get acquainted quickly, ask, "What are your disbeliefs?"

Don't rush to criticize others, there will be plenty for all.

Scientific progress is the discovery of new empirical questions.

Confident: *adj.* Oblivious to personal shortcomings.

Some of our most cherished memories are of places that we never visited, people we never knew, and events that preceded our births.

Having a plan gives the illusion of being in control.

Anarchy: *n.* A form of government administered by roving gangs of young men.

Psychological disorders have survived a long procession of thoughtful correctives: torture, exorcism, asylum, diagnosis, sterilization, lobotomies, electroconvulsive therapy, psychotherapy, and now "medication."

58

Why do both dogs and college students look at their teachers as though they are almost, but not quite, making sense?

Art by Anita Overton

Thinkers keep flapping their arms, expecting at any moment to lift off.

Children: *n. pl.* The barbaric hoards invading civilization.

Justice insures a fair trial, not a fair verdict.

A god who loses his believers is remaindered to mythology.

Everything is simple, so long as we are.

Most people are too busy living to just exist.

Your concerned heirs will caution you against wasteful spending.

Demagogue: *n.* A politician who refuses to let shame limit his aspirations.

A charitable eulogy for a malevolent person: "His ambitions were never realized."

Moslems and Christians worship the same God, the Hebrew God.

There are only two socio-economic classes: People who live beyond their means and people who live beyond their needs. The middle class is the area of overlap.

Euphemism: *n.* Respectable clothing for the naked truth.

The probability that Homo sapiens would evolve was infinitesimal, yet their extinction is certain.

Anti-intellectuals: *n. pl.* People who aren't necessarily uneducated but are sufficiently uneducated.

An aphorism says what the reader thinks it shouldn't.

Handling truth: The act of juggling
contradictions.

Ignorance: *n*. The precondition for learning.

The strongest link in the chain passes unnoticed.

Voters without a political party must think
before they vote.

Philosophers were motivated to contrive proofs
of the existence of God, not because they were
doubters but because they were believers.

64

People who survive into old age find that for the most part they didn't.

Art by G P Gardner

Plagiarism: *n*. Failure to acknowledge the author being misquoted.

Reliable: *adj*. The tendency to lose the same thing in the same place.

A shared smile reveals a shared understanding.

Organized people are just trying to manage their confusion.

A simple explanation can be correct, but only when it's a product of complex understanding.

Patriotism: *n.* Nationalism in its flag-waving adolescence, before it matures into goose-stepping adulthood.

Labor unions have two natural enemies: Angry employers and happy employees.

Scholars: *n. pl.* People who understand all that can be taught.

Intellectuals: *n. pl.* People who understand more than can be taught.

Psychopathy: *n.* The mental tranquility to transcend concern for the welfare of others.

Impertinence: n. Revenge of the powerless.

The most anomalous event in the universe was the evolution of a species that could understand the universe.

Art by Anita Overton

Old: *adj.* The state or condition in which a person is reminded of another story.

Autocrat: *n.* A politician who can accomplish everything he promises.

Mendacity: *n.* An insufficient regard for others.

People are easily embarrassed in their own language, and easily frightened in a foreign one.

Select with care the wall up against which you may be put.

The first to land receives more acclaim than the first to fly.

When we speak of others, we tell of ourselves.

Mind: *n.* A thinking spirit assigned to each person by philosophers who didn't realize that people could think for themselves.

Lovers: *n. pl.* Folie à deux.

Correct a mistake only when it wasn't an improvement.

Statesman: *n.* Someone who manages to leave high political office without attaining wealth.

After creating a language that conformed to the world, civilizations created a world that conformed to language.

Faith in immortality springs eternal.

A teacher can learn a lot from students, mostly irrelevant.

On the battlefield there is little discussion of patriotism.

Common sense: The wisdom of ignorance.

Wait until you are in a good mood to ask
yourself for forgiveness.

Retirement: *n.* When you finally have the time
to learn what you once needed to know.

The faster we change the world, the sooner we
can finish up.

To live in the moment, we must escape the
shackles of knowledge and understanding.

Astronomers transmit messages hundreds of light years into space, and then listen for a reply.

Freedom: *n.* Having no bridges left to burn.

Being lucky doesn't change the odds.

Ethanol: *n.* An over-the-counter oral medication that alleviates the symptoms of modesty and moderation.

We can never return to where we were, but we can always return from where we are.

Artists see the utility of science. Scientists see the beauty of art. Each misunderstands the other.

Arguing: *v.* Inoculating against a change of mind.

Compromise: *n.* A marriage of convenience between agreement and disagreement.

Liberal: *n.* Someone who thinks the government should be protected from the wealthy.

Conservative: *n.* Someone who thinks the wealthy should be protected from the government.

When quoting others, well-educated people can't resist making improvements.

Living a long time lengthens only your old age.

Art by Anita Overton

Life isn't fair; no one has to put up with himself.

Metaphysician: *n.* A philosopher who explains reality to scientists.

Anyone who is unable to avoid the opportunity can become a hero.

Dilettante: *n.* A trifler who goes to college just to get an education.

Because attempted murder requires less skill than murder, it carries a shorter sentence.

When men flirt they talk, when women flirt they just smile.

Ademonist: *n.* A skeptic who starts at the bottom.

Philosophers live in a world of words and ideas. It is left to scientists to hold their feet to the fire of reality.

Inventor: *n.* Henry Ford invented the automobile in 1896, too late to compete in the Paris to Rouen automobile race of 1894 or the Chicago Times-Herald automobile race of 1895.

In their hereafters, religions graciously provide accommodations for heretics.

Funerals attract only the living; the dead are forced to attend.

Professor: *n.* A person employed to provide rational answers to irrational questions.

What conceit! Atheists don't believe that there is an omniscient god who ordained their conception.

She was his window on the world. When darkness spread over her, he could see only himself.

Freedom of the press guarantees our right to speak; the right to be heard is left to the discretion of editors.

The boredom of good health is undervalued by the young.

Wisdom and knowledge are always gray; foolishness and ignorance come in garish colors.

Enjoyment of sex is the price we each must pay for being a member of a surviving species.

Age-old thoughts can be recognized by their rich patina and worn edges.

Politician: *n.* Someone who, when caught naked, announces that it's the latest fashion.

It's easier to pull liberals down out of the trees than to drag conservatives up out of the mud.

Art by G P Gardner

Arrogant: *adj.* Overconfident, overbearing, and
overabundant.

Make sure that the person you most admire is
someone else.

Renaissance man: A throwback to the 15th
Century.

Checks and balances: The U.S. Constitution
grants citizens the right to elect their leaders,
and assassins the right to bear arms.

We struggle to realize our dreams while we are
still young enough to destroy them.

Barbaric: *adj*. Absent the influence of educated women.

When the majority feels oppressed, minorities will be oppressed.

Cult: *n*. A religion whose immortal prophet is still alive and receiving contributions.

Life is the process of putting up with people you are going to miss.

Because we believe that all truths must agree, we search for agreeable truths.

In the competition to stay alive, heaven is the believer's booby prize.

Art by Susan Patton

Life is our last opportunity to understand.

Plan: *n.* Steps for rearranging the future.

As children we are shaped by our lives, as adults we shape our lives.

"Language exists" is a metaphysical proposition validated by its assertion—or denial.

It is easier to ask God for forgiveness than to ask those you harmed.

Good marriage: The union of two people, both giving more than they receive.

We each practice being our self, hoping one day to get it right.

Reading minds is not really that difficult, except for your own.

As the world spirals out of control, the elderly have time on their side.

Some states grant "the right to die," but only to citizens who can prove that they are dying.

Fear: *n*. An involuntary mental state that wards off the dangers of courage.

Art by Susan Paxton

We are told that faith is a virtue, but we soon learn that doubt is a greater virtue.

Capitalists: *n. pl.* Wealthy people who believe they earned it.

Most necessities aren't necessary.

"Every vote counts" is true only in elections decided by a single vote.

Journalism: *n.* A profession dedicated to insuring that the transient endures.

War: *n.* The necessary precondition for an era of peace.

Peace: *n.* The necessary precondition for an era of war.

Few people are liars, but everyone makes false statements.

Autodidact: *n.* A teacher who struggles to keep up with the only student in the class.

In a war between pacifists, there are still casualties.

Control is gained by asking questions and relinquished by providing answers.

The wisest person in the crosswalk is just another pedestrian in danger.

There have been many *theories* of evolution. Each provided an explanation of the *fact* of evolution.

In a house filled with fragile icons, careless people become iconoclasts.

Before you reject belief in the supernatural, prepare to face reality on its own terms.

Con man: Someone who, of professional necessity, earns your trust.

The highest form of understanding is human understanding, but few humans understand this.

The dying words of a well-educated man who was born in 1912 and had survived The Great Depression and World Wars I and II were "On the whole it was good."

How prayer works: When the storm comes, all parishioners pray to survive, and those who do survive thank God for His mercy.

Without belief in God, the search for truth never ends, and vice versa.

Making sense of the meaningless is easy but dangerous.

The more absurd the belief, the more confident the believers must be.

Art by Anita Overton

Wisdom may never stop asking the question that Ignorance will ask only once.

Aphorist: *n.* A writer who begins with a brief conclusion and then changes the subject.

We each search for the meaning of life. Those who find it are lost.

God created man, and man gratefully reciprocated.

Sustainable: *adj.* Requiring frequent maintenance (e.g., an old automobile or a new marriage).

Everything we know is from the past, even our knowledge of the future.

To want to be young again, one must be both old and foolish.

To both the poor and the rich, there are only two socioeconomic classes: The poor and the rich.

Oxymoron: *n.* An environmentalist with children.

Eloquence: *n.* An imposter masquerading as Knowledge.

If you can find no one to trust, someone you will trust may find you.

Fiancé: *n.* A person committed to the formalities of marriage and divorce.

Our best teachers made us educate ourselves.

Phony: *adj.* Not authentic.

Authentic: *adj.* [an archaic word with no modern meaning]

Wisdom reduces the ill effects of good intentions.

After the war ends, the winner, as well as the loser, struggles to recover from the loss.

Teacher: *n.* An educated person paid to keep company with people who aren't.

To see the face of God, just gaze at the heavens, but to see the heavens, stop looking for God.

The slam of the prison door is loudest on the inside.

Paranoid: *adj.* Appreciating the grandeur in one's self and the malice in everyone else.

Guru: *n.* A divine leader whose followers relinquish material wealth to obtain spiritual enlightenment.

Art by Susan Patton

Teachers explain the facts of science, professionals use the facts of science, but only researchers discover the facts of science.

People who no longer believe in truth may still believe that they know the truth.

Human knowledge is the scaffold we climb to construct ourselves.

Would people who seek eternal life settle for temporary death?

We get it wrong when we ascribe human motives to animals, and then again when we don't ascribe animal motives to humans.

A change of mind calls both positions into question.

If you're allowed to say that you don't have freedom of speech, then you probably do.

Almost everyone is wrong about almost everything, but apparently it doesn't matter.

Confusion: *n.* A receptive state of mind that heralds an opportunity to learn.

Even though life is all we know, we keep wondering what it is.

Love: *n.* A mindless attraction that matures into a mindful tolerance.

Most educated Americans don't know which war took the most lives. Most educated Europeans and Asians do.

The more we learn, the faster we can learn more.

Making reasonable decisions isn't evidence of freewill. It's the opposite.

Member: *n.* An individual who is required to answer for the actions of a group.

Hope: *n.* The belief that the inevitable will not happen.

Liberals think their country makes them free, so they should protect it.

Conservatives think they make their country free, so they should be protected from it.

The young want to be the first quadrupeds on the shore. The old just want to be the last dinosaurs in the swamp.

Failing health reassures the hypochondriac.

Creative: *adj.* Going the wrong way without getting lost.

The most environmentally friendly source of energy is unregulated nuclear power...ninety-three million miles away.

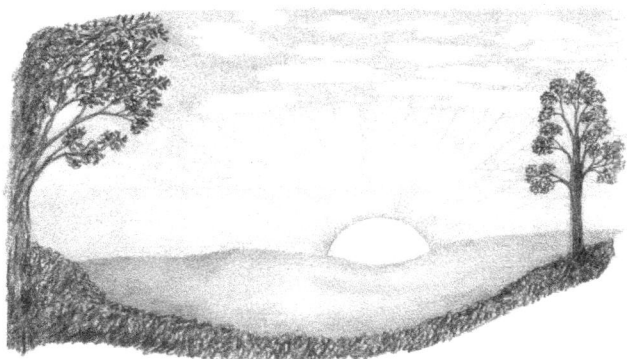

Art by Susan Patton

Everyone wants to be admired, but few want to live the kind of life that is admired.

A good education reveals how much we misunderstood, but not how much we still misunderstand.

Humans *evolved* language and self-awareness and then asked, "Why am I?" The answer can be found in the preconditions.

Not existing before birth bothers no one. Not existing after death bothers everyone.

Free market: A utopian economic system in which wages and prices are freed from the constraints of morality.

The falling leaves of common sense obscure the path to truth.

Hell: *n.* The petard on which Christian believers hoist themselves up to paradise.

Fulfillment: *n.* When dreams of the future have become memories of the past.

Miracle: *n.* The occurrence of an impossible event.

The light at the end of the tunnel may be the taillight of the train that you just stepped off of.

Life: *n.* A one-way trip with a seat by the window.

Dick Whittington Photography Collection

A kind epitaph for a modest person: "He left the world no worse than he found it."

If God created time, He has by now grown quite old.

For the wealthy desires are a product of incentives, but for the poor they are a product of deprivations.

To establish a new truth, you must first state it.

Europe: *n.* A mythical land inhabited by imaginary beings: Trolls, gnomes, elves, fairies, and Europeans.

Becoming a believer requires an open mind; remaining a believer requires it be closed.

"All the world's a stage. And all the men and women merely players...," and the finale for each is a disappearing act.

The road to liar's hell is paved with euphemisms.

We often quote, but seldom praise, Anonymous.

Integrity: *n*. Remaining true to yourself after everyone else has forgotten who you are.

We don't know where life is going, yet we don't want to be left behind.

Art by Susan Patton

Saying what you think is not "telling it like it is." It's telling it the way you are.

Theoretical physicist: A physicist more concerned with what might be than with what is.

Grace: *n*. Salvation for the graceless.

Bureaucrat: *n*. Someone who can create a rule for dealing with cases that don't fit any rule.

Spiritualists attribute natural events to invisible forces. Scientists do the reverse.

If I were you…. Never mind.

Why are beautiful people complimented for *being* beautiful?

People insist on making their own decisions, especially when they can't decide what to do.

Hospital: *n*. Where medical ceremonies are held for the departing soul.

Church: *n*. Where spiritual ceremonies are held for the departing body.

People often reject science when it contradicts the writings of the sacred scribes of the pre-soap era.

The toucan sees nothing unusual in the mirror.

Art by Susan Patton

Polite: *adj.* Suffering fools well.

How manners work: On the Titanic, men had
the good manners to let women go first into the
lifeboats, and women had the good manners to
accept the offer.

In the second half of the twentieth century,
American children began to ask, "What do I
want to do with my life?" Prior generations had
known what they had to do with theirs.

Patriot: *n.* A title traditionally assumed by
militants who oppose their government.

Eternity can have no end, except when it had no
beginning.

Birth: *n.* The end of our first eternity of oblivion.

The United States and the Soviet Union once prepared to fight a war that would destroy the world. The United States claims to have won.

Lust: *n.* A mental disruption that impels even those who know better to stop whatever they are doing and attempt to reproduce.

Leader: *n.* A charismatic person who doesn't know what can't be done.

Wisdom arises not from learning but from rational analysis of what we don't understand.

If I had lived a different life, then I wouldn't know about this one…. Wait, maybe this *is* the different one!

Plagiarizing yourself is not fraudulent, unless you are not the person you used to be.

Philosopher: *n.* Someone for whom an argument isn't a disagreement.

Scientist: *n.* Someone for whom a disagreement isn't an argument.

Education: *n.* The Sisyphean struggle to replace beliefs and opinions with facts and reason.

Democracy is the best form of government right up to the point a dictator is elected.

Wealth would be of little value if there were no poor people to hire.

Life is revealed only in hindsight, and fully revealed only in old age.

Destiny: *n.* An inevitable outcome that is brought about by its occurrence.

In each democracy, the hateful and ignorant restlessly await the coming of the demagogue.

A wealthy person is just an ordinary person with an extra zero at the end.

Medicine: *n*. Therapeutic poisons prescribed in sub-lethal doses.

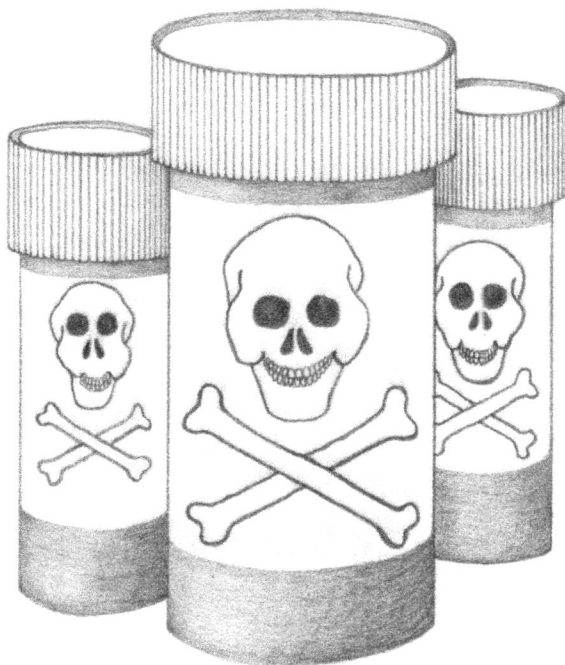

Art by Susan Patton

Transcendence is the most sublime expression of religion, worship the most ridiculous.

Archeologists observe current conditions of the earth in order to understand past events.

Astronomers observe past events in the universe in order to understand current conditions.

Democracy: *n.* A political lottery that lacks the benefit of random selection.

"KNOW THYSELF!" Beware, it's a trick—a command to do the impossible.

Most people are able to remain faithful to their spouse, while in view.

Logic: *n.* Arguing from premises to conclusions.

Rhetoric: *n.* Arguing from conclusions to premises.

Baby boomers grew old trying to decide what to do when they grew up.

People say what they think—in that order and in that person.

Wisdom: *n.* Understanding far more than is necessary.

Psychopath: *n.* Someone who gives his friends the opportunity to be more useful.

Pure genius is anonymous.

Celebrate, you exist! What were the odds?

Lucky: *adj*. Having finally won.
Unlucky: *adj*. Having finally lost.

Martyrdom: *n*. A demonstration that myths of death are stronger than facts of life.

Well-adjusted: *adj*. Comfortable with your shortcomings.

If time should reverse, little would change,
unlearning would just replace forgetting.

"I'm a workaholic," admitted the alcoholic
during the job interview.

To survive, the essential need be only adequate,
whereas the inessential must be excellent.

Only a chump would fall for an *ad hominem*
argument.

If you don't decide what to do with your life,
your life will decide what to do with you.

Many who lived a full life died young.

Art by Anita Overton

Dr. Z was neither a scholar who knew everything, nor a genius who understood everything. He was just a skeptic who understood what he knew.

Quickly correcting a mistake invites mistakes.

We live just this side of eternity.

Scientific facts can always be corrected, that's why they seldom need corrected.

If you believe a human zygote is a person, you're counting your chickens before they hatch.

We avoid disaster by deferring to experts. We court disaster by impersonating them.

All insults written on the border wall can be erased, except one: "Keep Out."

An oppressive state inspires only poets and assassins.

Everyone is in a hurry, but only the well educated move with dispatch, alacrity, or haste.

Nihilist: *n.* A zealot in his formative years.

Existence: *n*. The temporary absence of oblivion.

Art by Anita Overton

For the thinker, the assertion of any opinion implies, "On the other hand...."

Arguments result from opposing credulities.

Like great music, great lives are improvisations on a familiar theme.

Our lives didn't really begin until long after we were born, and they may end long before we die.

We can begin our search for truth once we realize that almost everything we've learned is wrong.

Taking offense serves no useful purpose. It restrains only the considerate.

To cover his bets, Pascal should have wagered that *all* gods exist.

Book: *n.* An invitation to a conversation with someone who doesn't listen.

Mr. B was modest and unassuming, but he hoped no one would notice.

Some days seem endless, yet eternity passes in an instant, unnoticed.

Virtual: *adj.* Synthetic, but without substance.

For most of us, each day begins with an unwelcome resurrection and ends with a welcome death.

The purpose of life is the same for every thinker, to transcend life.

Everyone is taken seriously when speaking about death, but only a poet is taken seriously when speaking about life.

Freewill: *n.* The ability to make decisions without relevant information.

Mastery of the language makes facile explanations possible. Mastery of the subject matter makes them impossible.

To deceive, we alter truth. To mislead, we omit truth. To persuade, we disregard truth.

Law: *n.* A clever system established by the old and weak to control the young and strong.

Only gods and gullible people think they see the world as it is.

If we could see the future, we wouldn't value the present.

Despot: *n.* Someone destined to go down in history and take a nation with him.

Art by Anita Overton

The man who believes that he and he alone can understand his motives is wrong on both accounts.

It's good to still be alive, not that we will notice the difference.

Childhood: *n.* That developmental period in which failure is still funny.

Agnostics! Which gods remain on your list of possibilities and which ones are just too ludicrous?

They were a lucky couple, each better than the other deserved.

All ego defense mechanisms are logical fallacies.

We are destined to follow the plans of those who came before.

Repeated failures free us from the confines of competence.

In a world of spirits, a physical universe would be unimaginable.

We don't understand life because we can't imagine its opposite.

The young believe they know the right paths;
the old believe they know the wrong paths.

Election: *n.* A process of governmental change
by which the wealthy purchase the honor of the
candidates thereby freeing them to exploit the
credulity of the poor.

There are two sides to every argument. The
critic's mandate is to discover how both are
wrong.

The poor and the wise form a natural political
bond to oppose the inevitable coalition of the
rich and the simple.

148

AUTHOR

William Melvin Gardner was born in Birmingham, Alabama, in 1940 and grew up at his family's farm on Lassiter Mountain. He served in the USAF and then earned a Ph.D. in Experimental Psychology from the University of Alabama, Tuscaloosa. He taught graduate and undergraduate psychology courses at Jacksonville State University and conducted research in comparative psychology, learning, sensory disorders, and academic cheating. Since retiring, he has written articles on automotive history and compiled the *Encyclopedia of Eight-Cylinder Engines*. He is best known for his book *Handling Truth: Navigating the Riptides of Rhetoric, Religion, Reason, and Research* (2012, rev. 2020). He lives with his wife, mystery novelist G. P. Gardner, in a small town on Mobile Bay.

williammelvingardner.com

150

BIBLIOGRAPHY

Auden, W. H. and Kronenberger, Louis
    The Faber Book of Aphorisms: A Personal Selection
    Faber and Faber Limited (1962)

    The Viking Book of Aphorisms: A Personal Selection
    Barnes and Noble Books (1966,1993)

Bierce, Ambrose
    The Cynic's Word Book
    Doubleday, Page, & Company (1906)

    The Devil's Dictionary
    Neale (1911)
    The World Publishing Company (1941)
    Dover Publications, Inc. (1958)
    University of Georgia Press (2017)

    The Collected Writings of Ambrose Bierce
    The Citadel Press (1946)
    Carol Publishing Group (1989)

Chazal, Malcolm de
    Pensées, Volumes I-VII
    The General Printing & Stationery Cy Ltd *(1940-1945)*

    Pensées et Sens-Plastique
    The General Printing & Stationery Cy Ltd (1945)

    Sens-Plastique, Volume II
    The General Printing & Stationery Cy Ltd (1947)
    Gallimard (1948)

    Sens-Plastique (Translated by Irving Weiss)
    Herder and Herder (1971)
    Sun (1979)
    Green Integer (2008)

Geary, James
> *The World in a Phrase: A Brief History of The*
> *Aphorism*
> Bloomsbury (2005)
>
> *Geary's Guide to the World's Great Aphorists*
> Bloomsbury (2007)

Gross, John
> *Oxford Book of Aphorisms*
> OUP (1983)

Guida, James
> *Marbles*
> Turtle Point Press (2009)

Hoffer, Eric
> *The True Believer: Thoughts on the Nature of Mass*
> *Movements*
> Harper Perennial (1951)
>
> *The Passionate State of Mind ~ and other aphorisms*
> Buccaneer Books (1955)

JPJ
> *Last Aphorisms*
> Self-published (2009)

Khayyam, Omar
> *Rubaiyat of Omar Khayyam* (Translated by Edward
> FitzGerald)
> Houghton, Mifflin & Co. (1887, 1888, 1894)
> Jaico Publishing House (1948)

Lababidi, Yahia
> *Signposts to Elsewhere: A book of aphorisms, epigrams, maxims and other tailored thoughts*
> Sun Rising Press (2006)
> Jane Street Press (2008)
>
> *Where Epics Fail: Meditations to Live By*
> Unbound (2018)

La Rochefoucauld, François duc de
> *Réflexions, ou Sentences et maximes morales*
> Chez Claude Barbin (1665)
>
> *Maxims* (Translated by Leonard Tancock)
> Penguin Books (1959)

Lavater, Johann Kaspar
> *Aphorisms on Man, Fifth Edition* (Translated by Henry Fuseli)
> Mackay Croswell & Co. (1795)

Lec, Stanislaw J.
> *Myśli nieuczesane*
> Wydawnictwo Literackie (1957)
>
> *Unkempt Thoughts* (Translated by Jacek Galazka)
> St Martin's Press (1962)
>
> *Myśli nieuczesane nowe*
> Wydawnictwo Literackie (1964)
>
> *More Unkempt Thoughts* (Translated by Jacek Galazka)
> Funk & Wagnalls (1968)

154

Lichtenberg, Georg Christoph
Vermischte Schriften
Lichtenberg's sons and brothers (1800)

Aphorisms (Translated by R. J. Hollingdale)
Penguin Books (1990)

Lough, James and Stein, Alex, Editors.
*Short Flights: Thirty-Two Modern Writers Share
Aphorisms of Insight, Inspiration, and Wit*
Schaffner Press, Inc. (2015)

Murray, George
Glimpse: Selected Aphorisms
ECW Press (2010)

Nash, Ogden
Verses from 1929 On
Random House (1952)

Pascal, Blaise
Pensées
Chez Guillaume Desfrez (1670)

Pensées (Translated by Joseph Walker)
Joseph Walker (1668)

Pensées (Translated by W. F. Trotter)
E.P. Dutton (1958)
CreateSpace Independent Publishing (2011)

Porchia, Antonio
Voces
Self-published (1943)

Voices (Translated by W. S. Merwin)
Big Table Publishing (1969)
Alfred A. Knopf (1988)
Copper Canyon Press (2003)

Richardson, James
> *Vectors: Aphorisms & Ten-Second Essays*
> Ausable Press (2001)
>
> *Interglacial: New and Selected Poems & Aphorisms*
> Ausable Press (2004)
>
> *By the Numbers*
> Copper Canyon Press (2010)

Taleb, Nassim Nicholas
> *The Black Swan*
> Random House (2007)
>
> *The Bed of Procrustes: Philosophical and Practical Aphorisms*
> Random House (2010).

Turovsky, Mikhail
> *Зуд Мудрости*
> Цикута (1981)
>
> *Itch of Wisdom* (Translated by Edmund Levin and Lilia Rogovaya)
> Hemlock Press (1990)